UNDERSTANDING JOLLY PHONICS: A COMPREHENSIVE GUIDE TO EARLY LITERACY

DR DHEERAJ MEHROTRA

Contents

Preface

Childhood literacy is the foundation for lifelong learning, curiosity, and success. Jolly Phonics, a phonics-based reading and writing program for young children, has recently gained popularity. This method emphasises sound-letter links and uses entertaining, multi-sensory methods to make learning fun and successful for kids.

Understanding Jolly Phonics: A Comprehensive Guide to Early Literacy is an accessible resource for teachers, parents, and carers who want to promote early reading. This book demystifies Jolly Phonics with clear explanations, practical recommendations, and real-life examples.

This handbook can help you improve your teaching and support your students, whether you've been using Jolly Phonics for years or not. The book teaches Jolly Phonics fundamentals, from sound recognition and blending to advanced tactics for teaching difficult words. Each chapter provides helpful techniques to help children acquire confidence as they start reading.

Remember that early literacy inspires a love of reading, language, and communication, not only teaching letters and sounds. May this guidance help you build a nurturing, engaging, and thriving learning environment where every child can succeed in literacy and beyond.

Welcome to Understanding Jolly Phonics: A comprehensive guide to early literacy. May it start a joyful journey of influencing young brains.

Author

www.authordheerajmehrotra.com

Jolly an
Phmis

ONE
INTRODUCTION TO JOLLY PHONICS

Introduction to Jolly Phonics?

Jolly Phonics is a fun, child-centred approach to teaching literacy through synthetic phonics. Developed by Sue Lloyd and Sara Wernham, the method emphasizes learning the sounds of letters rather than their names. This is important because when children learn to read, recognizing sounds (phonemes) is more beneficial than focusing solely on the alphabetical order or names of letters.

The Importance of Phonics in Early Childhood Education is foundational to literacy development. It enables children to decode words, the first step toward fluency in reading. Phonics teaches children the relationships between the sounds of spoken language and the written symbols that represent them. In a language as complex as English, phonics gives children the tools to understand how words are constructed, improving reading comprehension and spelling.

Jolly Phonics presents this concept in a multi-sensory, interactive way that suits young learners. Children can better retain and recall what they learn by incorporating actions, stories, and songs with each letter sound.

Overview of the Jolly Phonics Method Jolly Phonics is structured around 42 main sounds of English, grouped into seven sets of six sounds. These sounds cover the full spectrum of the English alphabet and digraphs (two letters that make one sound, such as 'sh' or 'ai'). The method uses a multi-sensory approach, meaning children engage in auditory, visual, and kinesthetic learning activities catering to different learning styles.

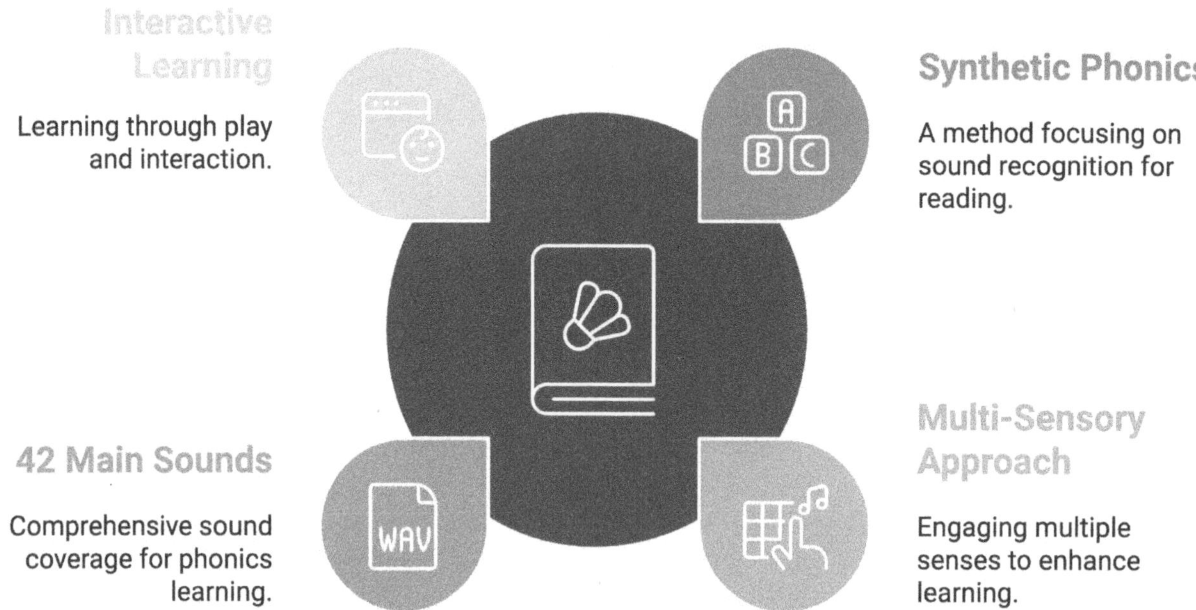

Using a synthetic phonics approach, Jolly Phonics teaches children the five key skills for reading and writing. The programme continues through school enabling the teaching of essential grammar, spelling and punctuation skills.

TWO
WHAT IS JOLLY PHONICS?

The core of the Jolly Phonics method focuses on developing five essential literacy skills:

Learning the Letter Sounds: Children are introduced to the 42 main sounds of English, including single letters and digraphs.

Letter Formation: Teaching children how to write letters correctly using multi-sensory techniques.

Blending: Combining individual sounds to form words. This is essential for developing reading fluency.

Segmenting: Breaking words down into their component sounds for spelling.

Tricky Words: These are words that cannot be sounded out phonetically. They must be learned by sight.

The multi-sensory, action-based approach makes learning these skills enjoyable, engaging, and effective for early readers.

Conclusion:

Understanding Jolly Phonics and integrating it into early education helps build a strong foundation for literacy. This comprehensive guide explores the method's components, tips for effective teaching, and the impact on early childhood learning. Educators can use Jolly Phonics to ensure their students have the necessary tools to become confident, proficient readers and writers.

Understanding Jolly Phonics: A Comprehensive Guide to Early Literacy

This document is a comprehensive guide to Jolly Phonics, an innovative and effective approach to teaching early literacy skills to young learners. Jolly Phonics focuses on phonics, the relationship between sounds and their corresponding letters, providing children with the foundational skills necessary for reading and writing. This guide will explore the principles, methods, and benefits of Jolly Phonics and practical tips for educators and parents to implement this approach in their teaching practices.

What is Jolly Phonics?

Jolly Phonics is a systematic phonics program for children aged 3 to 7. It emphasizes teaching 42 letter sounds, including the alphabetic letters and digraphs (two-letter combinations that make one sound). The program uses a multi-sensory approach, incorporating actions, songs, and stories to engage children and enhance their learning experience.

Jolly Phonics Overview

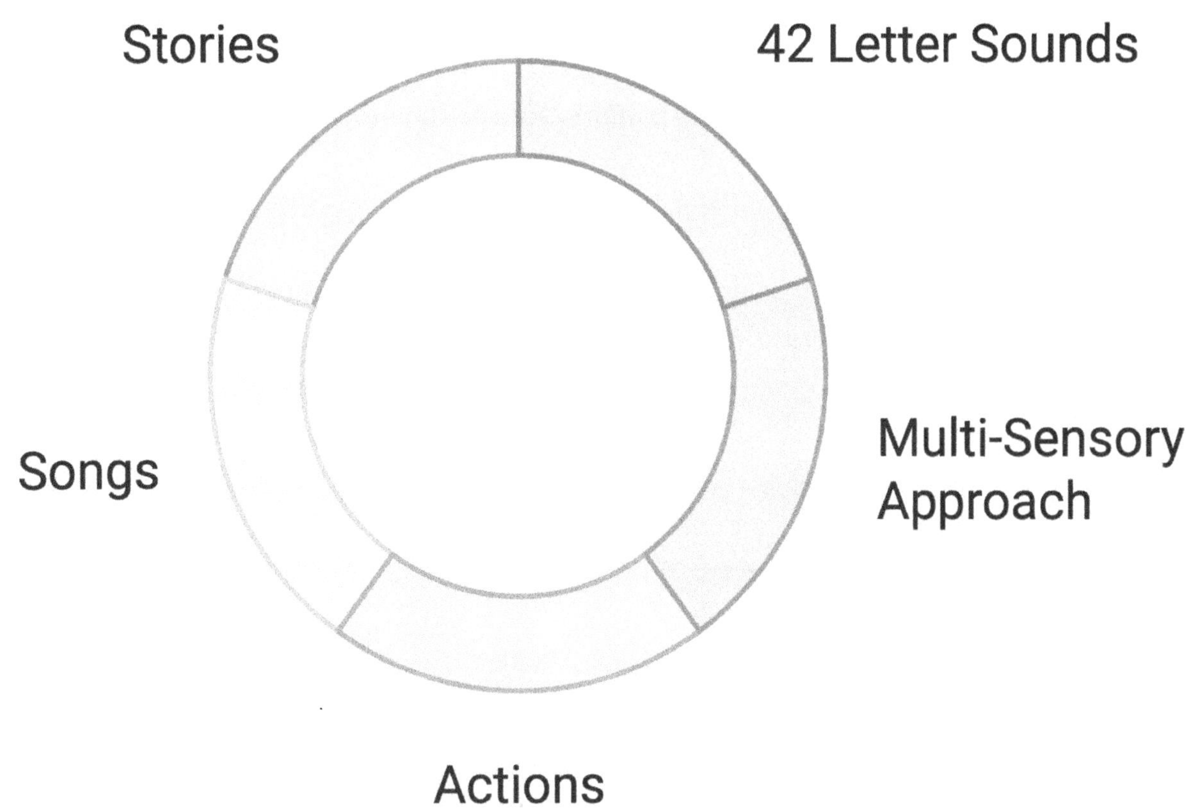

The benefits of the early introduction to literacy through Jolly Phonics include:

Improved cognitive development

Improved confidence & self-esteem

Enhanced emotional and social skills

Better chance of academic success in school and occupational success after school

Improved oral communication and motor skills

An overall love for reading, writing and learning

Critical Components of Jolly Phonics

1. The 42 Sounds

Jolly Phonics introduces children to 42 sounds grouped into seven sets. Each sound is taught with a corresponding action, making it easier for children to remember and recognize them. The sounds include:

Set 1: s, a, t, i, p, n

Set 2: c, k, e, h, r, m, d

Set 3: g, o, u, l, f, b

Set 4: ai, j, oa, ie, ee, or

Set 5: z, w, ng, v, oo, oo

Set 6: ar, or, ur, ow, oi, ear

Set 7: air, ure, er

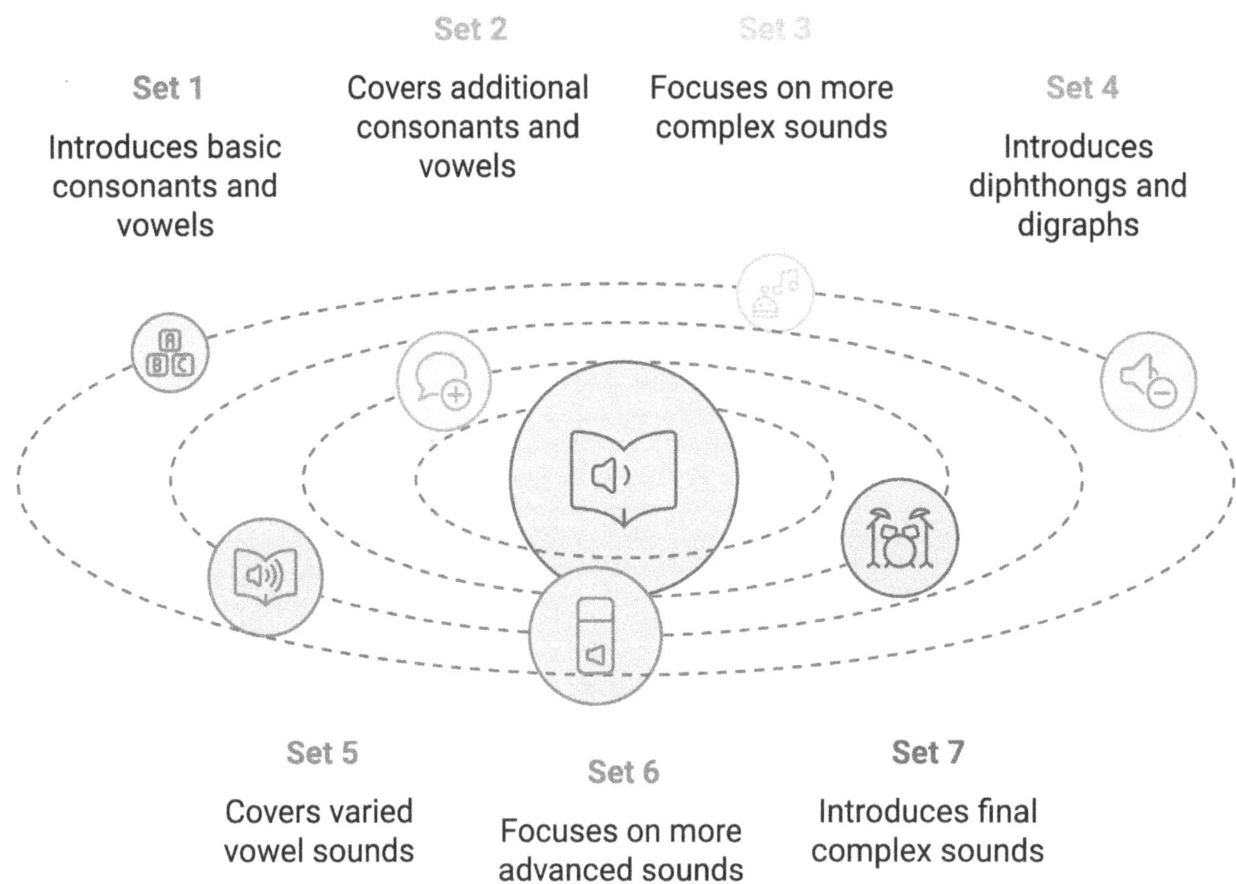

2. Blending and Segmenting

Blending and segmenting are crucial skills in phonics. Blending involves combining individual sounds to form words while segmenting breaks down words into their constituent sounds. Jolly Phonics teaches these skills through various activities and games, helping children to develop their reading and spelling abilities.

Developing Reading and Spelling Skills

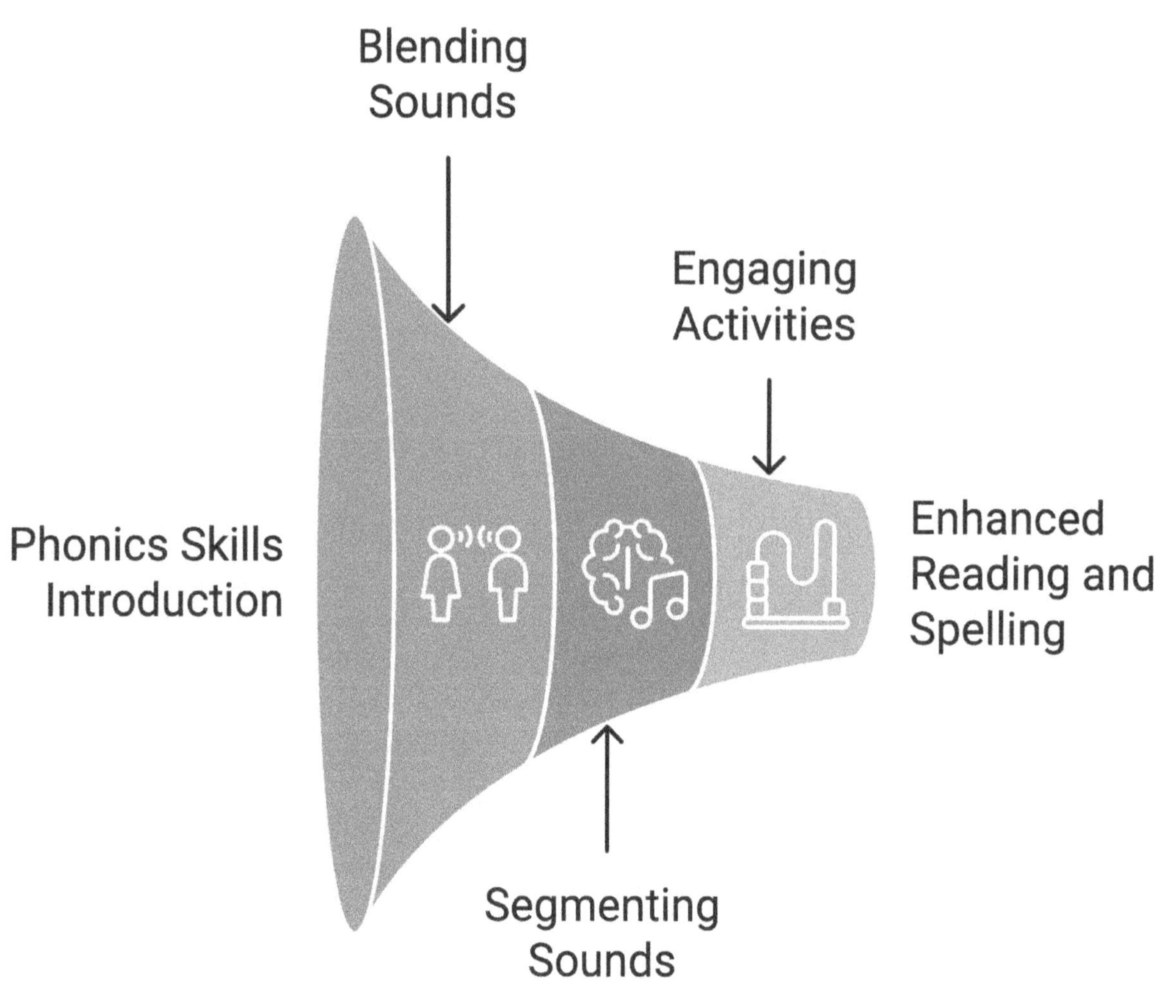

3. Tricky Words

In addition to phonics, Jolly Phonics introduces "tricky words" that do not follow standard phonetic rules. These words are taught through repetition and practice, enabling children to recognize them in reading and writing.

How to teach children to recognize "tricky words"?

Phonics-based

Teaches children to sound out words using phonetic rules.

Repetition and Practice

Teaches children to recognize tricky words through repeated exposure.

Benefits of Jolly Phonics

Engagement: The multi-sensory approach keeps children engaged and motivated to learn.

Foundation for Literacy: Jolly Phonics provides a strong foundation for reading and writing, equipping children with essential skills.

Confidence: As children master phonics, they gain confidence in their reading abilities, fostering a love for books and learning.

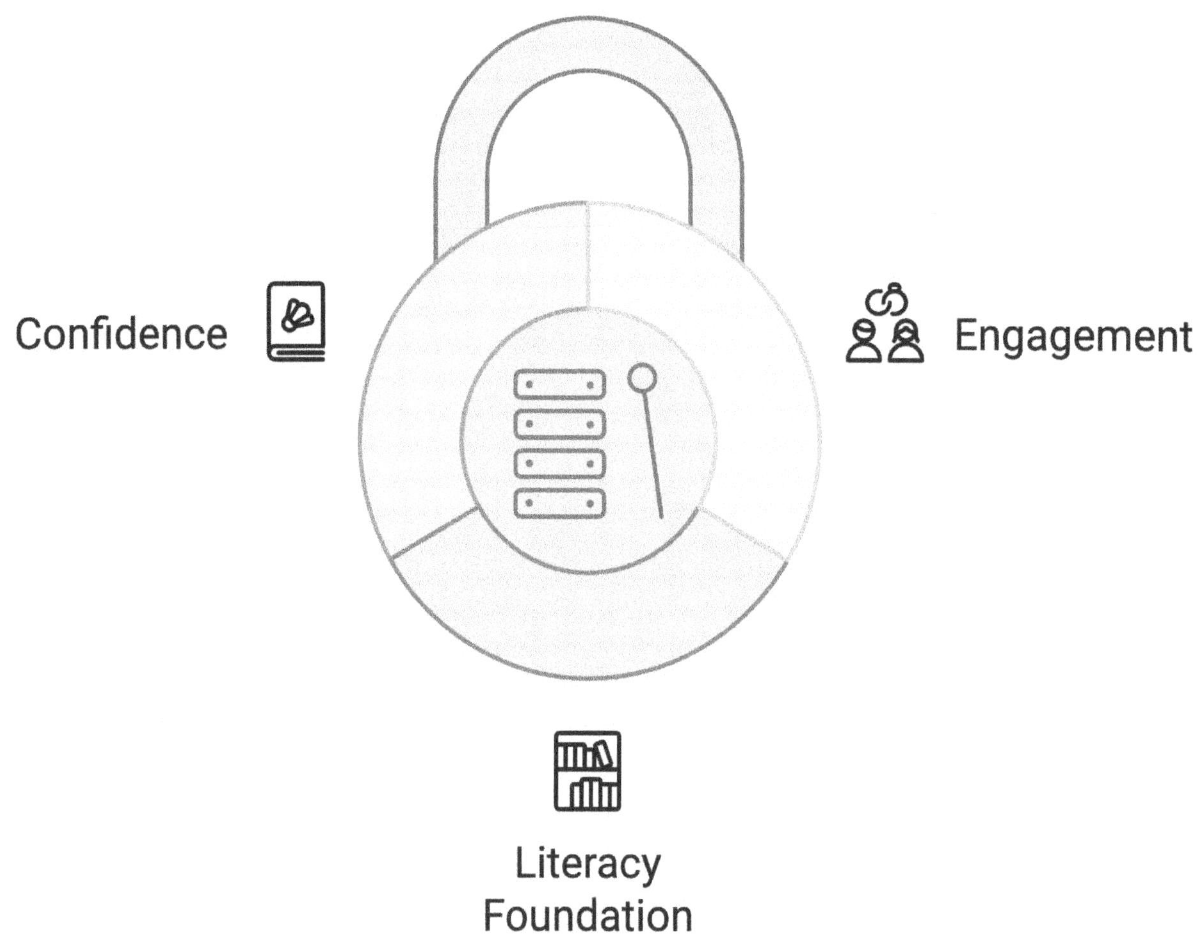

Practical Tips for Implementation

Use Multi-Sensory Techniques: Incorporate actions, songs, and visual aids to reinforce learning.

Create a Phonics-rich Environment: Surround children with print, labels, and phonics resources to encourage exploration.

Practice Regularly: Consistent training is vital to mastering phonics. Incorporate short, daily phonics sessions into your routine.

Encourage Reading: Provide access to various books and encourage children to read aloud.

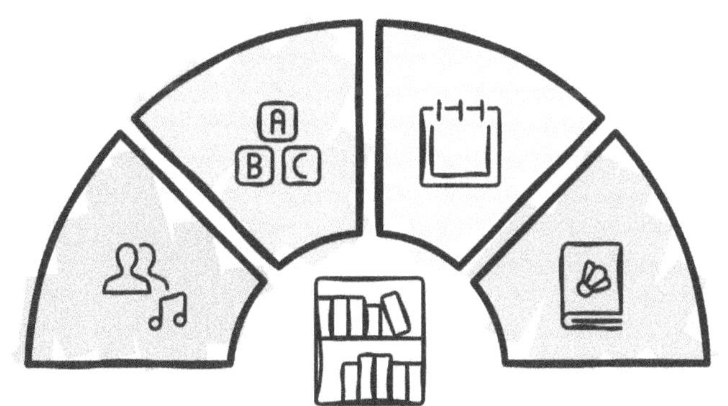

Conclusion

Jolly Phonics is a powerful tool for teaching early literacy skills, providing children with the foundation for reading and writing. By understanding its principles and methods, educators and parents can effectively implement this approach, fostering a love for literacy in young learners. With its engaging and systematic framework, Jolly Phonics has the potential to transform the way children learn to read and write, setting them on a path to lifelong learning.

THREE

IMPORTANCE OF PHONICS IN EARLY CHILDHOOD EDUCATION

The five basic skills emphasized in Jolly Phonics are:Learning the letter sounds.Letter Formation.Blending.Identifying sounds in words.Spelling irregular or `tricky' words (said, was, the, etc.).

Importance of Phonics in Early Childhood Education

Phonics is crucial in early childhood education, serving as a foundational element for literacy development. This document explores the significance of phonics in helping young learners decode words, improve reading fluency, and enhance overall language skills. By understanding the importance of phonics, educators and parents can better support children's reading journeys and foster a love for learning.

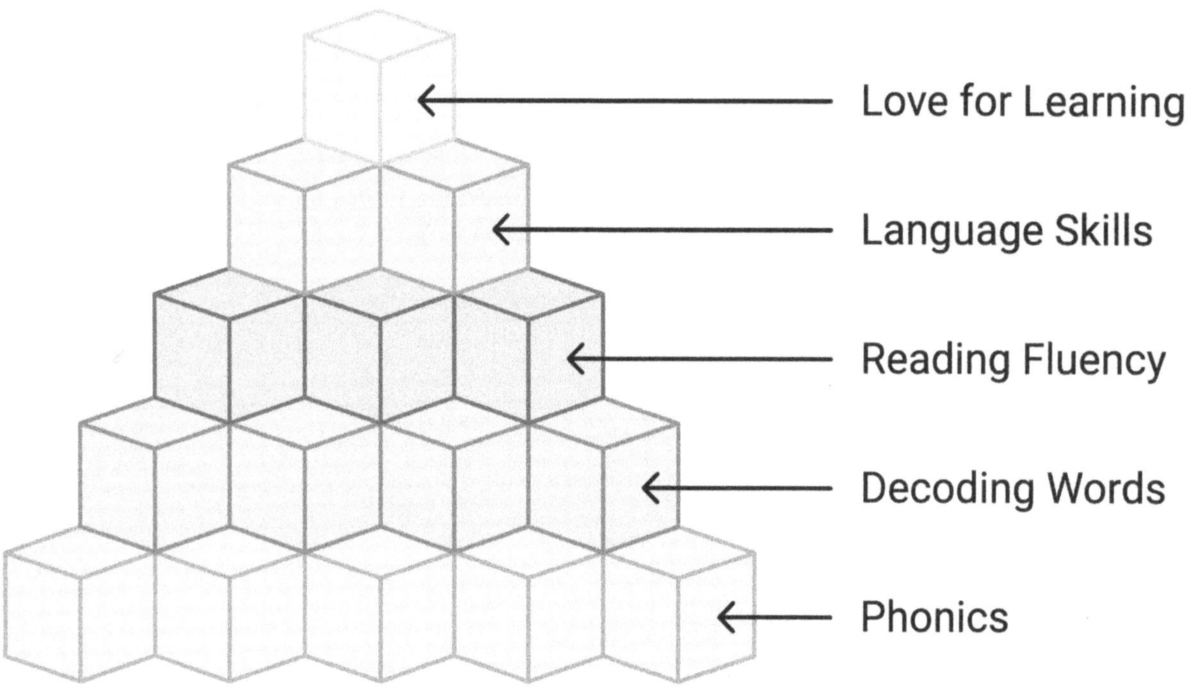

Understanding Phonics

Phonics is a method of teaching reading and writing that focuses on the relationship between sounds and their corresponding letters or groups of letters. It involves teaching children to recognize the sounds of letters and how these sounds combine to form words. This systematic approach enables children to decode unfamiliar words, making reading a more accessible and enjoyable experience.

Phonics Learning Structure

Combinations of letters forming meaning

Written symbols representing sounds

Basic auditory elements of language

Core method for reading and writing

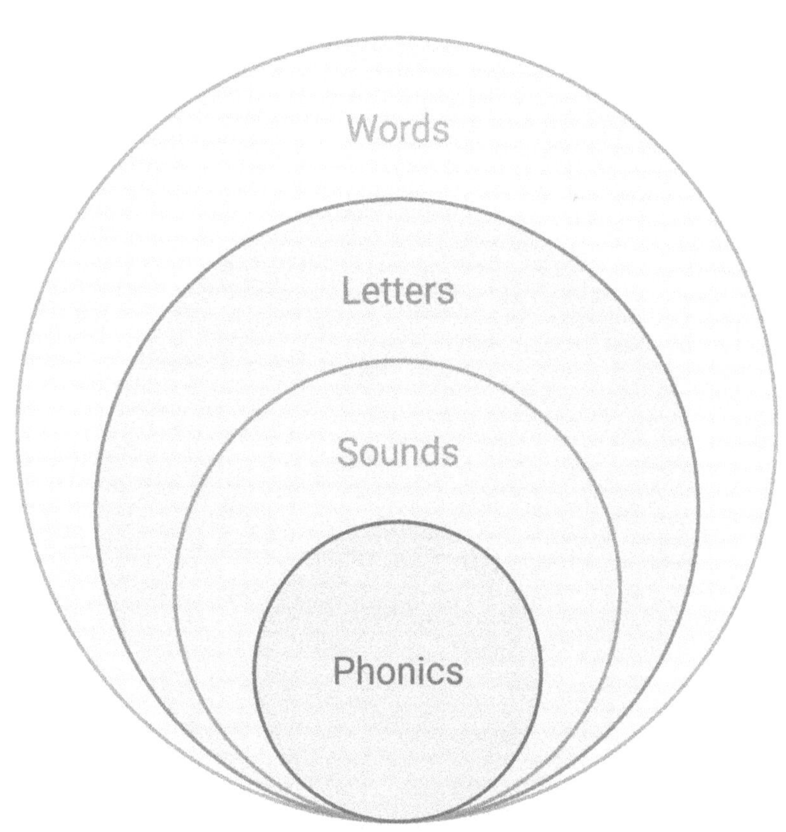

Enhancing Reading Skills

One of the primary benefits of phonics instruction is its ability to enhance reading skills in young children. Children can break down words into manageable parts by learning the sounds associated with letters, allowing them to read independently. This skill is essential as it lays the groundwork for more complex reading tasks and comprehension skills.

Reading Skills Development

Building Vocabulary

Phonics not only aids in decoding words but also contributes to vocabulary development. As children learn to read, they encounter new words and concepts, which expands their language repertoire. A strong phonics foundation enables children to tackle a broader range of texts, increasing their exposure to diverse vocabulary and enhancing their overall language proficiency.

Building Vocabulary through Phonics

Enhanced Language Proficiency

Achieving a high level of language skills

Expanding Language Repertoire

Broadening the range of known words and concepts

Encountering New Words

Meeting and learning new vocabulary

Decoding Words

Developing the ability to read and understand words

Phonics Foundation

Establishing a strong phonics base for reading

Improving Spelling Abilities

Phonics instruction also significantly improves spelling abilities. Children can apply this knowledge to spell words correctly by understanding the sounds that letters represent. This connection between phonics and spelling reinforces learning as children practice reading and writing simultaneously.

Journey to Enhanced Spelling

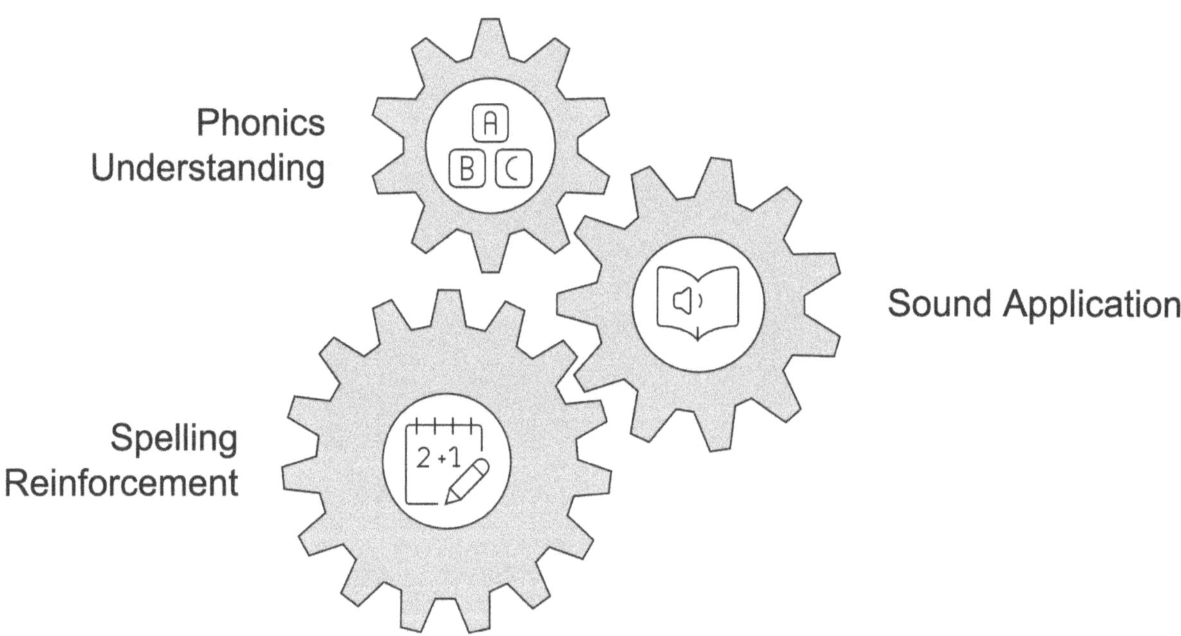

Fostering a Love for Reading

When children grasp phonics principles, they gain confidence in their reading abilities. This newfound confidence can foster a love for reading, encouraging children to explore books and stories independently. A positive reading experience in early childhood can lead to lifelong habits of reading and learning, ultimately benefiting their academic and personal growth.

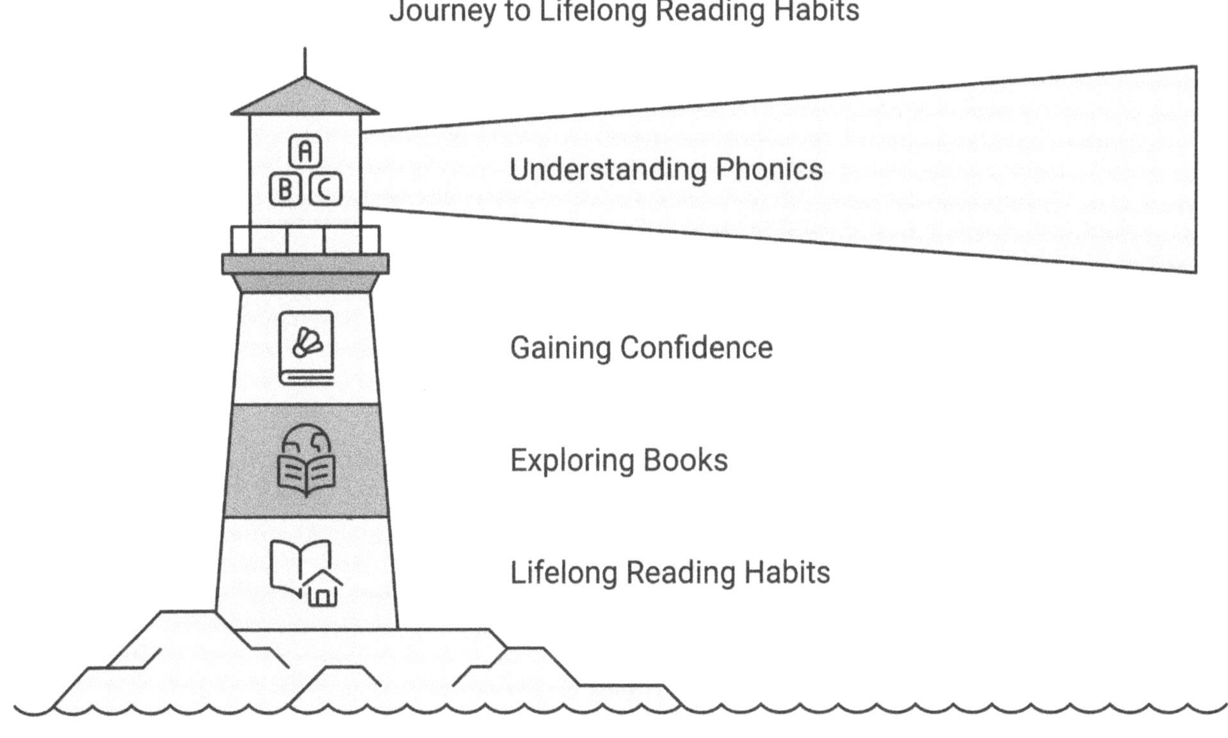

Conclusion

In conclusion, phonics is an essential component of early childhood education that significantly impacts children's literacy development. Educators and parents can equip young learners with the necessary skills to decode words, build vocabulary, improve spelling, and cultivate a passion for reading by focusing on phonics. Emphasizing phonics in early education enhances literacy skills and sets the stage for future academic success.

FOUR

OVERVIEW OF THE JOLLY PHONICS METHOD

Anc

Jolly Phonics is a phonics program that teaches children how to read and write using a systematic approach to phonics. The program starts with the letter s because it is one of the most common and useful letters in the English language.

Overview of the Jolly Phonics Method

The Jolly Phonics Method is a systematic and multi-sensory approach to teaching reading and writing to young children. It emphasizes phonics, the relationship between sounds and their corresponding letters, making it an effective tool for early literacy development. This document provides an overview of the Jolly Phonics Method's key components, principles, and benefits, highlighting its significance in early childhood education.

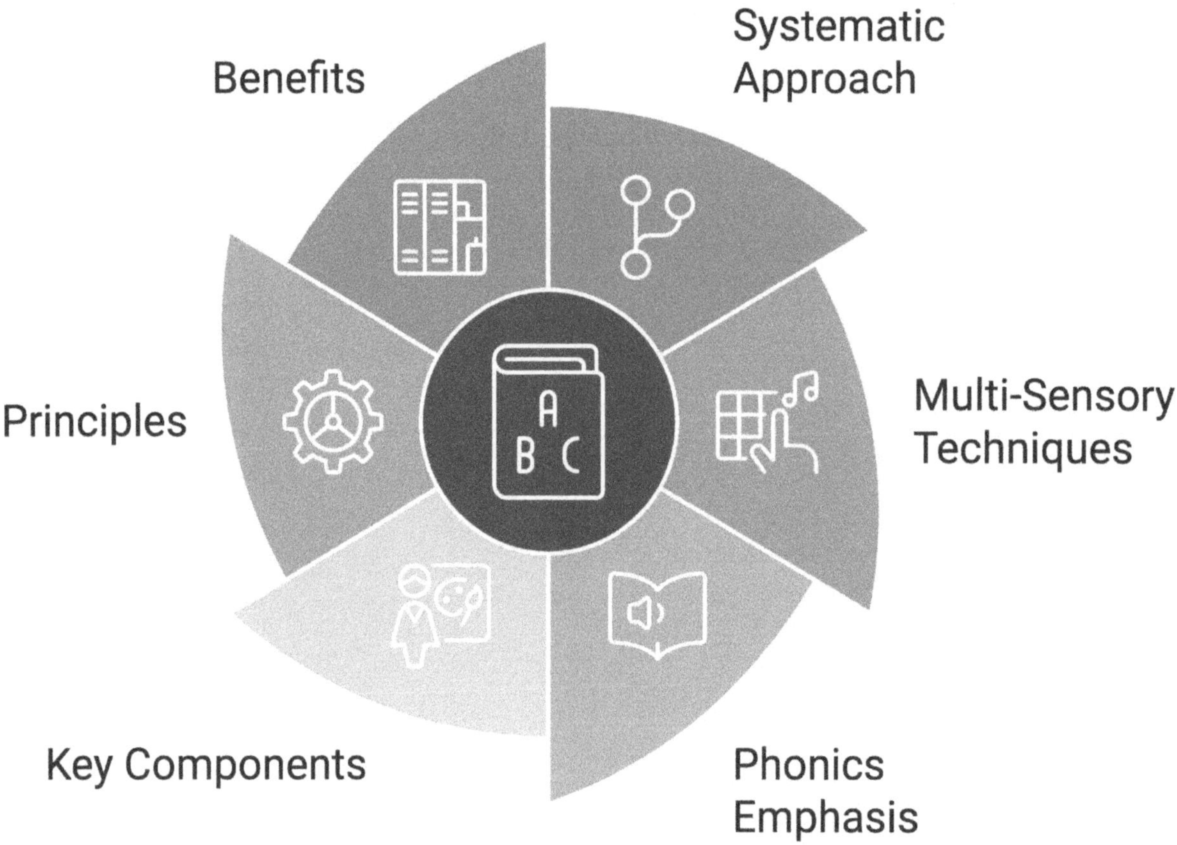

Key Components of Jolly Phonics

Phonics Instruction: Jolly Phonics introduces children to the 42 letter sounds of the English language, including digraphs (two letters that make one sound, like 'sh' and 'ch').

Multi-Sensory Learning: The method incorporates visual, auditory, and kinesthetic activities to engage children. For example, children learn sounds through songs, actions, and stories, making learning enjoyable and memorable.

Blending and Segmenting: Children are taught to blend sounds to read words and segment sounds to spell them. This foundational skill is crucial for developing reading fluency and writing proficiency.

Tricky Words: Jolly Phonics also introduces 'tricky words' that do not follow standard phonetic rules. These words are taught alongside phonics to help children recognize them in context.

Storybooks and Resources: The method is supported by various storybooks, worksheets, and resources that reinforce the phonics skills learned in class.

Components of Jolly Phonics

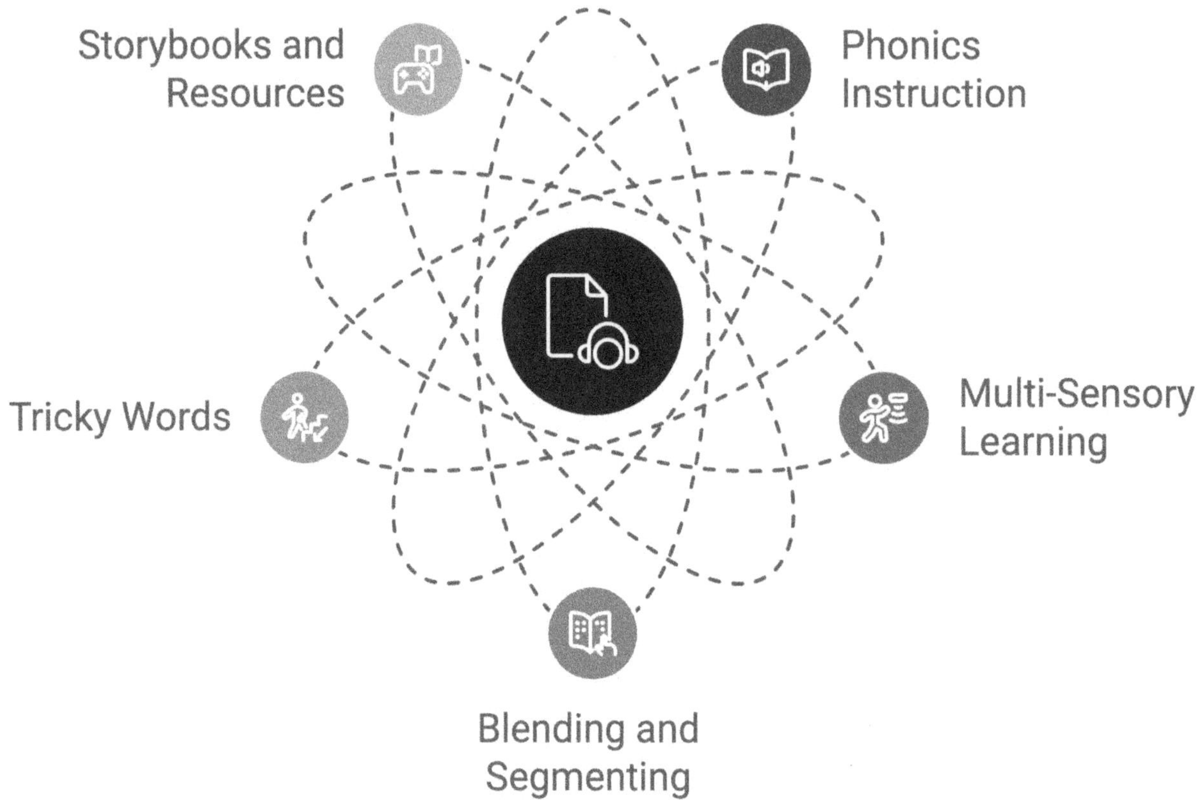

Principles of Jolly Phonics

Child-centred learning encourages children to participate in their education, fostering independence and confidence actively.

Sequential Progression: Skills are taught logically, allowing children to build on their knowledge progressively.

Inclusive Approach: Jolly Phonics is designed to cater to different learning styles and abilities, making it accessible to all children.

Benefits of Jolly Phonics

Improved Literacy Skills: Research has shown that children learning through the Jolly Phonics Method often achieve better reading and writing outcomes than those learning through traditional methods.

Engagement and Motivation: The program's interactive and fun nature keeps children engaged, making them more likely to enjoy learning.

Foundation for Future Learning: Mastering phonics strengthens children's foundation for future literacy skills, including comprehension and vocabulary development.

Achieving Literacy Success with Jolly Phonics

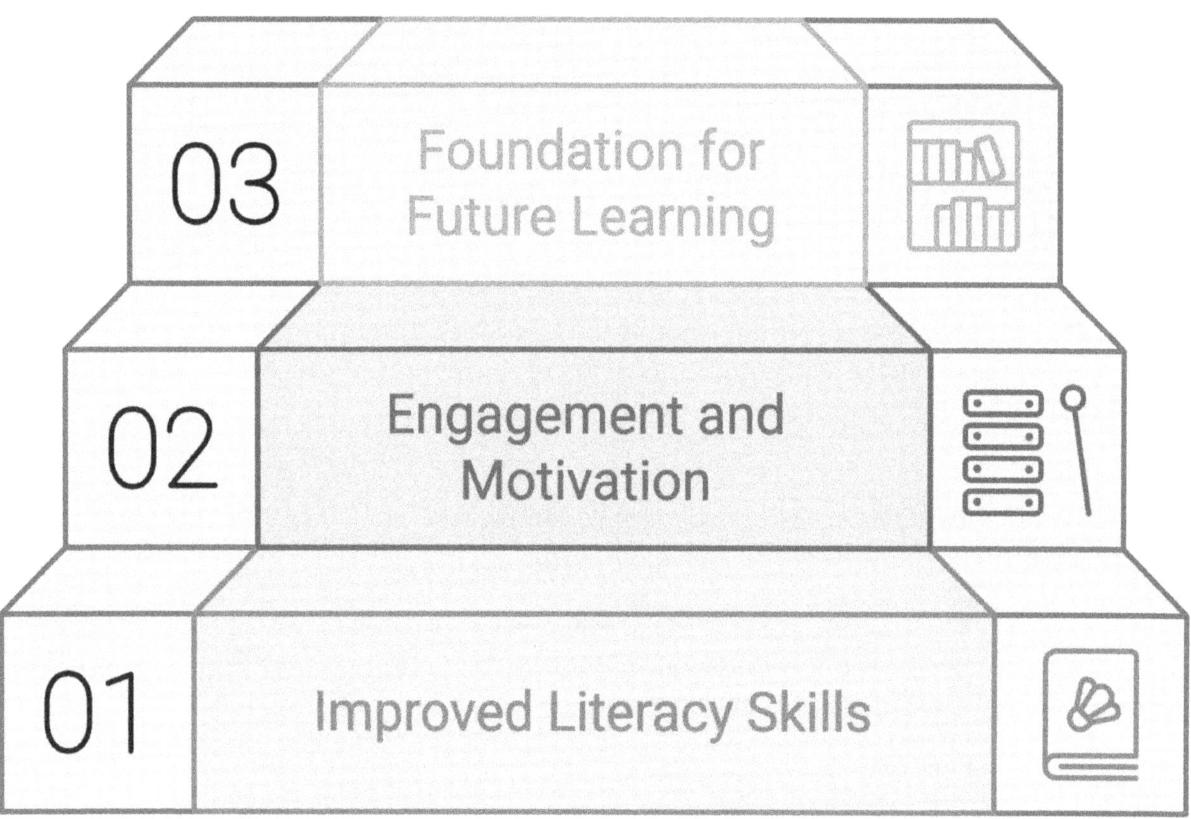

Conclusion

The Jolly Phonics Method is a comprehensive and practical approach to teaching literacy to young learners. Focusing on phonics, multi-sensory learning, and child-centred principles equips children with the essential skills they need to become confident readers and writers. As educators and parents seek effective strategies for early literacy, the Jolly Phonics Method stands out as a valuable resource in fostering a love for reading and writing from an early age.

FIVE

THE 5 KEY SKILLS IN JOLLY PHONICS

Jolly Phonics teaches using a variety of techniques and includes audio, visual, kinesthetic and tactile activities and exercises throughout. As a result, it can be a very effective choice for students with different learning styles and homeschools that place an importance on engaging, multisensory learning.

The 5 Key Skills in Jolly Phonics

Jolly Phonics is a systematic and multi-sensory approach to teaching reading and writing, primarily aimed at young children. This method emphasizes the importance of phonics, enabling children to decode words and develop their literacy skills effectively. In this document, we will explore the five key skills that form the foundation of the Jolly Phonics program, providing insights into how each skill contributes to a child's reading and writing development.

Foundations of Jolly Phonics

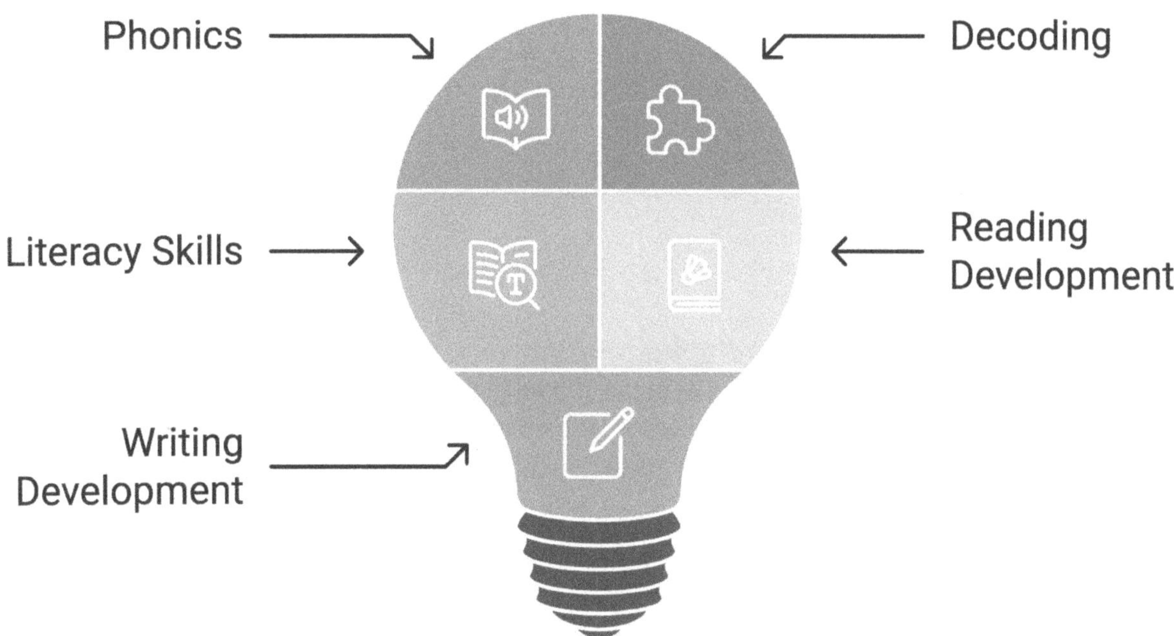

1. Learning the Letter Sounds

The first skill in Jolly Phonics involves teaching children the sounds associated with each alphabet letter. Instead of focusing solely on the letter names, children learn the sounds that letters make. This foundational skill is crucial as it allows children to blend sounds to form words. For example, knowing that the letter 's' makes the /s/ sound helps them read and write simple words like "sat" and "sun."

2. Learning Letter Formation

Once children are familiar with the sounds, the next step is to teach them how to form the letters correctly. This skill involves both handwriting and the physical aspect of writing. Children learn to write letters in a way that is both legible and consistent. Proper letter formation is essential for developing good writing habits and ensuring children can express their thoughts clearly.

3. Blending

Blending is the skill of combining individual sounds to read words. In Jolly Phonics, children practice blending sounds to decode words they encounter. For instance, when they see the letters 'c', 'a', and 't', they learn to blend these sounds to read the word "cat." This skill is vital for reading fluency and comprehension, enabling children to tackle new words independently.

4. Segmenting

Segmenting is the reverse blending process and involves breaking down words into their sounds. This skill is essential for spelling, as it helps children identify the sounds they hear in words and translate them into written form. For example, when asked to spell "dog," children learn to segment words into /d/, /o/, and /g/. Mastering segmenting allows children to become proficient spellers and enhances their literacy skills.

5. Tricky Words

The final key skill in Jolly Phonics is the recognition of tricky words, which are words that do not follow standard phonetic rules. These words, such as "the," "said," and "was," often cannot be sounded out using phonics alone. Teaching children to recognize these words by sight is crucial for developing reading fluency. Children can read more smoothly and confidently by incorporating tricky words into their vocabulary.

Jolly Phonics Learning Sequence

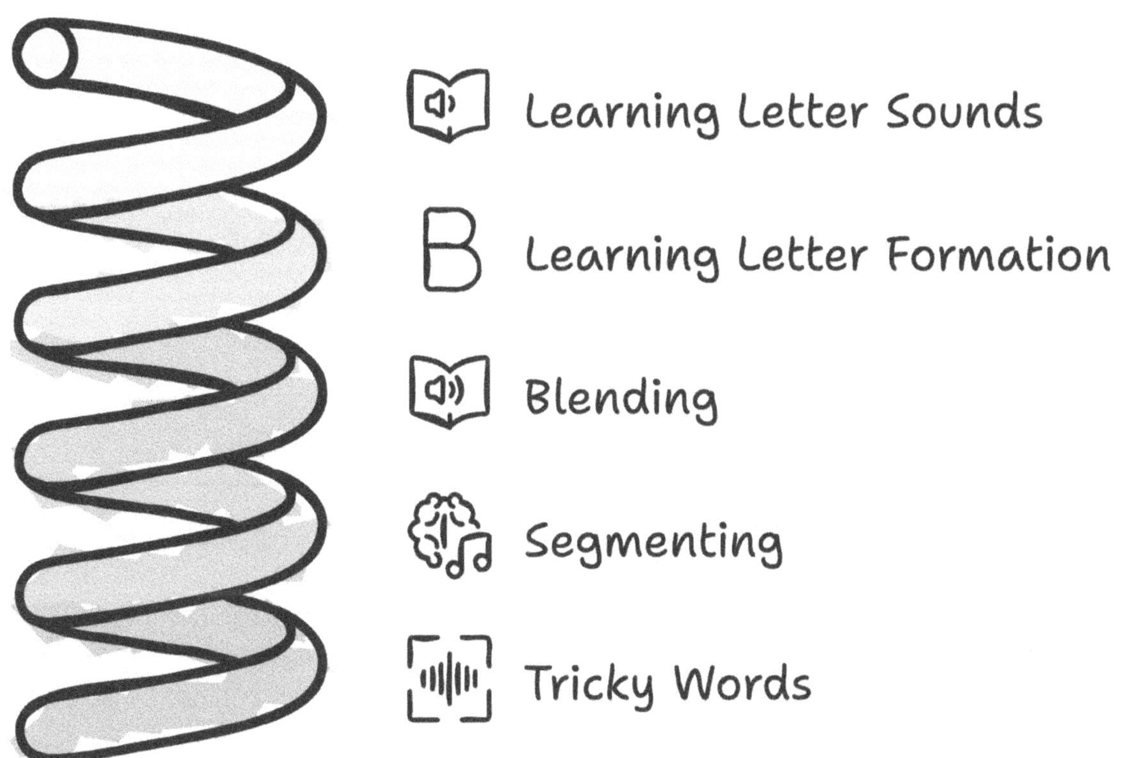

Conclusion

The five key skills in Jolly Phonics—learning letter sounds, letter formation, blending, segmenting, and recognizing tricky words—are essential to early literacy education. By focusing on these skills, educators and parents can provide children with a strong foundation in reading and writing, setting them up for success in their academic journey. Embracing the Jolly Phonics approach makes learning fun and empowers children to become confident and capable readers and writers.

SIX

Teachers' Tips For Teaching Jolly Phonics

Comprehending the Jolly Phonics System

Jolly Phonics is a phonics program aimed to teach children the 42 letter sounds used in the English language from a systematic perspective. It emphasizes the significance of phonemic awareness, the mixing of sounds, and the segmentation of words. This program employs a multi-sensory approach, including songs, actions, and tales, to make learning enjoyable and memorable for the participants.

Instructors and students can have an exciting and fulfilling experience teaching Jolly Phonics. The following tips offer a variety of valuable suggestions and methods for successfully executing the Jolly Phonics curriculum in the classroom. These strategies enable educators to establish an interactive educational setting that cultivates phonemic awareness and literacy abilities in students who are still in the process of learning.

Effective Jolly Phonics Teaching Strategies

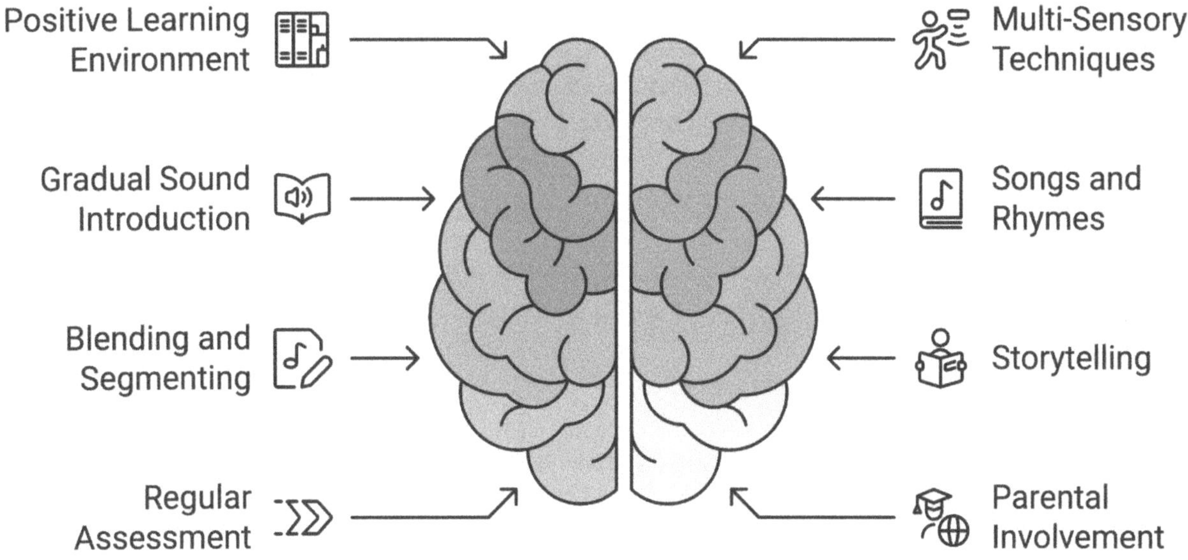

Jolly Phonics is a reading programme based on systematic synthetic phonics approach and developed by Sue Lloyd and Sara Wernham, who were practising classroom teachers at Woods Loke Primary School in Lowestoft, England and is published by Jolly Learning, UK that is owned by Christopher Jolly.

Here are some practical tips for teaching Jolly Phonics to young learners:

1. Establish an Emotionally Supportive Educational Setting

It is essential to create an encouraging environment so that the students feel safe asking questions and making mistakes. Positive reinforcement can help achieve success and encourage engagement. Use techniques that use several senses. To accommodate various learning styles, visual, aural, and kinaesthetic activities should be incorporated. Incorporating interactive games, puppets, and props can make lessons more engaging.

3. Gradually Add Sounds to the Environment

Start with a few sounds each week and ensure kids have mastered them before going on to the following sounds. If you use the Jolly Phonics movements, students will have an easier time remembering the sounds connected with each letter.

4. Incorporate Rhymes and Songs into the Mix

Use Jolly Phonics songs to reinforce sounds and make learning fun. Encourage pupils to sing along and perform movements to improve their ability to remember information.

5. Acquire experience in blending and segmenting

Blending sounds to make words and breaking words down into their component sounds should be practised regularly. Before moving on to more challenging vocabulary, using easy-to-understand and familiar words is vital.

6. Storytelling

It is helpful to read stories that incorporate the sounds taught to reinforce learning in context. Encourage children to write their own stories, utilising the sounds they have learnt.

7. Conduct Assessments regularly

Informal assessments are conducted to track students' progress and comprehension levels. Playing games and participating in activities is a pleasant and low-pressure way to evaluate a student's phonics skills.

8. Include a Parent or Carer in the Discussion

Sharing materials and ideas with parents is essential to reinforcing learning at home. Encouraging parents to read to their children and practise working with sounds together is also essential.

9. Exert tolerance and adaptability.

It is essential to recognise that every child learns at their own pace, and you should be ready to modify your instructional strategies accordingly. Keep kids motivated and involved by celebrating even the smallest of their triumphs.

10. Continuing Education and Training for Professionals

Ensure you are current with Jolly Phonics resources and instructional methods. Participate in workshops and work together with members of the teaching community to exchange ideas and experiences.

11. Teach the letter sounds: Start by systematically introducing the 42 letter sounds of the English language.

12. Teach letter formation: Once the letter sounds are introduced, teach children how to form each letter correctly.

13. *Teach letter names: After introducing the letter sounds and formations, teach the letter names associated with each sound.*

14. *Teacher's letter actions and songs.*

15. *Introduce blending and segmenting.*

16. *Teach tricky words.*

17. *Introduce alternative spellings and digraphs.*

18. *Continue with regular practice.*

19. *Use Actions and Songs.*

20. *Use Visual Aids.*

21. *Use Hands-on Activities.*

22. *Introduce sounds in a logical sequence.*

23. *Encourage Blending and Segmenting Early*

24. *Teach Tricky words separately.*

25. *Use Games and Interactive Activities.*

26. *Incorporate Daily Practice.*

27. *Encourage Repetition and Practice with New Words.*

28. *Model Enthusiasm and Positivity.*

29. *Provide Individual Support and Feedback.*

30. *Read Aloud Together.*

31. *Involve Parents.*

32. *Incorporate Individual Pacing.*

33. *Explore Small Group Instructions.*

34. *Use Technology and Digital Tools.*

35. *Create a Phonics-Friendly Classroom Environment.*

36. *Encourage Sound Exploration with Manipulatives.*

37. *Introduce Phonological Awareness Activities like Rhyming Games and Syllable Clapping.*

38. *Incorporate Movement with Learning.*

39. *Leverage Storytelling and Creative Writing.*

40. *Regular Assessment and Progress Tracking.*

41. *Promote Peer Learning and Group Activities.*

42. *Practice Phonics Across the Curriculum.*

43. *Use Repetition Wisely.*

44. *Provide Real-World Reading Opportunities.*

45. *Keep Phonics Fun and Playful.*

46. *Incorporate Storybooks that Reinforce Phonics Skills.*

47. Create a phonics-rich Home-School Connection.

48. Use Art and Craft Activities to Reinforce Sounds.

49. Implement Phonics "Stations" for Independent Practice.

50. Engage Children in Sensory Activities like Character for Each Sound and puppet Practice.

Working with children to teach them Jolly Phonics may be a rewarding experience that significantly impacts their literacy skills. Educators can cultivate young readers by establishing a dynamic and efficient learning environment by implementing the earlier guidelines and tactics. It is important to remember that the secret to success rests in making learning exciting and participatory. This will ensure that kids acquire a love for reading and writing that will live on for the rest of their lives. Remember to make the learning experience fun and interactive by incorporating games, activities and resources from the Jolly Phonics program. Adopt the pace and activities based on your students.

About The Author

Dheeraj Mehrotra, a white and a yellow belt in SIX SIGMA, a Certified NLP Business Diploma holder, is an Educational Innovator, Author with expertise in Six Sigma In Education, Academic Audits, Neuro-Linguistic Programming (NLP), Total Quality Management In Education, an Experiential Educator, a CBSE Resource towards School Assessment (SQAA), CCE, JIT, Five S, and KAIZEN. He has authored over 100 books on computer science, AI, digital body language, NLP, quality circles, school management, classroom effectiveness, and safety and security. A former Principal at De Indian Public School, New Delhi, (INDIA), NPS International School, Guwahati, Kunwar's Global School, Lucknow and an Education Officer at GEMS, Gurgaon, with ample teaching experience of over Three Decades, he is a certified Trainer for Quality Circles/ TQM in Education and QCI Standards for School Accreditation/ School Audits and Management. He has also been honoured with the President of India's National Teacher Award in 2006 and the Best Science Teacher State Award (By the Ministry of Science and Technology, State of UP), among others. He has published over 100 books and developed 150 FREE EDUCATIONAL MOBILE Apps for the Google Play Store exclusively for Teachers, Students, and Parents. This work has been recognised by the LIMCA BOOK OF RECORDS and INDIA BOOK OF RECORDS as the only Indian to draw that feast. As a premium UDEMY Instructor, he has developed over 500 courses and caters to over 8 Lakh students from 180 countries. As a founder and president of the IoT Society of India, he also promotes Technology Globally. Dr Mehrotra is presently engaged as a REGIONAL HEAD of the GEMS EDUCATION India Region.

ON THE ROCKS
ON THE ROCKS
HENRY
ROCKS
ROCKS

Books By The Same Author

www.authordheerajmehrotra.com